Intertwined
Daily
Inspirations

Alisha Kay Goodman

Copyright © 2023 Alisha Kay Goodman

All rights reserved.

ISBN: 9798859555468

DEDICATION

All Glory to God, by his Holy Spirit, for giving me the words, and the confidence to author this book. I appreciate the love and support from my husband Randy Goodman, sons Luke & Seth Goodman, and twin sister Trina Stokes. I love you all so much.

MY PRAYER FOR YOU

Dear God, I pray that your words and Spirit will dwell in each reader's heart as they read this book, and they will feel you speak to them. They will remain in you and trust you are with them every day. In Jesus' name, Amen.

GIVE US THIS DAY

Give us this day our daily bread.
Matthew 6:11

Universally known as the Lord's prayer in Matthew Chapter 6, "Give us this day our daily Bread," is a striking articulation in the bible. We see this articulation all over the place; however, have we at any point halted to grasp what this verse is saying? Every Day, we should ask God for his supply, as we cannot be sure about tomorrow.

So, you have woken up today breathing; these are the primary words that should come from your mouth. God, give me this Day; I need you. God has made this day, and knowing God is our daily source helps us to trust it is all in His hands. He sustains us every Day. If we can grasp that it is in Jesus that we live and breathe, then we will understand asking Him each morning to give us this Day. It is our daily priority. He is with us minute by minute and hour by hour!

Prayer: My God, give me this day, my daily bread. Help me rest in you, knowing that you have given me everything I need for my life today. In Jesus' name, Amen.

Date 11-27-23

What I am thankful for

today: Jesus + The Cross + His Resurrection, today and every day and all Day long.

My personal

Prayer: To be more like Jesus!

WHOLEHEARTED

You will seek me and find me when you seek me with all your heart.
Jeremiah 29:13

Living wholeheartedly for the Lord is impossible in our strength. But if we humble ourselves and ask, He will give us the grace to live for Him diligently and persistently. What is the significance of being wholehearted towards God? Being wholehearted is not about doing everything right but understanding the posture of our heart towards Jesus.

The verse above says we will find him when we seek him. It should motivate us to surrender any area that needs God. Are you attempting to tackle life's problems alone? Do you have things in your daily life causing you to sin? Seek Jesus with your whole heart today and ask Him to clean your life so that you will be pleasing to him. As you seek him, he has promised that you will find him. There is nothing more satisfying in life than to live it for Jesus. Give him your whole heart today! Psalm 51:10

Prayer: My God, I give my life over to you and want you to be first in all that I do. Please change me as I seek you with my whole heart. In Jesus' name, Amen.

*Date*_____

What I am thankful for

today:__Jesus, Jesus, Jesus!_____

_____

_____

_____

_____

_____

_____

_____

My personal

Prayer:_____

_____

_____

_____

_____

_____

_____

_____

ONLY BELIEVE

Then Jesus told him, "Because you have seen me, you have believed; blessed are those who have not seen and yet have believed."

John 20:29

The word "believe" is in the Bible multiple times, primarily in the New Testament. Belief is the hardest thing to make sense of, yet everyone wants to have something to believe in. The belief that Jesus is speaking of in the verse above is a simple solicitation, yet the most moving thing for an individual to do. The world treats this word like a value we can accept or reject. It fights against our human nature to trust in something we cannot see. The Bible verse above expresses that blessings come by belief without seeing Jesus with our own eyes.

The enemy of this world wants to keep us from believing in Jesus, but Jesus wants us to believe in him so he can shower us with his love. By believing in Jesus, who died on the cross to forgive sins, we can have eternal life in heaven and experience God's power in our lives even without seeing Him. Will you choose to believe today without seeing?

Prayer: My God, thank you for cherishing me; I believe and trust in you even if I cannot see. Help me serve you with my life.
In Jesus' name, Amen.

*Date*_____

What I am thankful for

today:_____

_____

_____

_____

_____

_____

_____

_____

My personal

prayer:_____

_____

_____

_____

_____

_____

_____

_____

MASTER PLANNER

But the plans of the Lord stand firm, the purposes of his heart through all generations.

Psalm 33:11

I found a job opening for a "Master Planner" at a pharmaceutical company while browsing through job listings. The job description had words like "owning," "supporting," and "monitoring," which made me curious, so I clicked to read more. Immediately, I thought of our God, the *Master Planner!* Jeremiah 29:11 states: "For I know the plans I have for you," declares the Lord, plans to prosper you and not to harm you, plans to give you hope and a future. I have seen his plans play out in my life over and over.

Our Lord is omnipotent, able to do anything, and omniscient, our all-knowing God. The Bible says in Jeremiah 1:5 that He knew us before birth. The plans of the Lord stand firm. He will fulfill his purpose through each one of us. Our job description is to trust the plan he created for us. His plans are always better than our plans. He is the Master Planner!

Prayer: My God, thank you that you are the Master Planner, and you know the plans you have for me. Help me relinquish control, rest in your arms, and allow you to direct my steps today.
In Jesus' name, Amen.

*Date*_____

What I am thankful for

today:_____

_____

_____

_____

_____

_____

My personal

prayer:_____

_____

_____

_____

_____

_____

_____

MORE GRACE

The law was brought in so that the trespass might increase. But where sin increased, grace increased all the more.
Romans 5:20

We all have a sinful nature that can put us in unpleasant and troubling circumstances. God was aware of our continual need to seek forgiveness before Jesus came to die on the Cross for our sins. God sacrificed his one and only son on the Cross because he loved us deeply. If you know Jesus, no sin is so great that he will not cover it with grace. Do you need to feel His forgiveness? Have you hurt someone's feelings, acted selfishly, or done something you regret? This is where more grace comes in.

No matter if you believe you deserve grace or not. Jesus has freely given grace through the power of His resurrection on the Cross. His grace washes away our human impurities as much as needed. His grace saves us from ourselves and helps us in every moment of our day, and his grace is more than enough!

Prayer: My God, thank you for expressing your mighty love for me by dying on the Cross. I can live freely by your grace and presence in my life. Help me grasp that your grace is enough.
In Jesus' name, Amen.

*Date*_____

What I am thankful for

today:_____

_____

_____

_____

_____

_____

_____

My personal

prayer:_____

_____

_____

_____

_____

_____

_____

_____

BRANDED BY THE FAMOUS ONE

From now on, let no one cause me trouble, for I bear on my body the branding marks of Jesus.
Galatians 6:17

When you think of famous fashion designers, do you think how nice it is to wear their brand name on your clothing for all others to see? Flaunt it and show people you have the money to purchase such lovely items. The quality of the brand name is also essential; if it is a brand from Walmart that costs much less, people usually think less of it, and the product usually will only last for a while. But if it is a brand like Gucci, Louis Vuitton, or Calvin Klein, then the quality based on price would be much more significant. Cattle ranchers also brand their livestock to show those to whom they belong. Branding is a significant cultural phenomenon.

Accepting Jesus means belonging to Him as a priceless gift, thanks to the high value He paid for us on the cross. You are marked, branded by the most famous one, Jesus, for the entire world to see.

Prayer: My God, I believe in you. Forgive me of my sins and be the Lord of my life. You have branded me with your marks. I want my life to exemplify you so others will want to know you, too.
In Jesus' name, Amen.

*Date*_____

What I am thankful for

today:_____

_____

_____

_____

_____

_____

_____

My personal

prayer:_____

_____

_____

_____

_____

_____

_____

WHY CRUMBLE

Why do you call me, 'Lord, Lord,' and do not do what I say? As for everyone who comes to me and hears my words and puts them into practice, I will show you what they are like. They are like a man building a house, who dug down deep and laid the foundation on rock. When a flood came, the torrent struck that house but did not shake it because it was well-built.
                                                              Luke 6:46-48

Life's storms can shake us and make us feel like we will crumble at any moment. Have you ever thought about the foundation of a home or building? When building, the contractors must appropriately install the concrete and footings. So that when storms, earthquakes, and rain come, the foundation will not crack, and the building will withstand, be stable, and not crumble. Strong foundations will remain firm even under the hardest of life's seasons. We all know influential people who have gone through harsh life storms, but they always hold it all together, make it through, and become stronger.

The Bible emphasizes the importance of a solid foundation based on obedience to God's word to withstand challenging times. Applying God's principles in our lives is the building block. The next time you go through a big life storm, you can weather it and not crumble because your foundation is on the word of God.

Prayer: My God, help me build my foundation upon your words so that I will be firm when the storms of life come. I trust in you that I will be victorious through all life's storms.
In Jesus' name, Amen

*Date*_____

What I am thankful for

today:_____

_____

_____

_____

_____

_____

_____

My personal

prayer:_____

_____

_____

_____

_____

_____

_____

HE IS ABOVE ALL

The one who comes from above is above all; the one who is from the earth belongs to the earth and speaks as one from the earth. The one who comes from heaven is above all.

John 3:31

Humans, by nature, are interested in what is happening around them; they see the problems in the world, relationships, health, work, finances, and unfair life conditions. The temptation to control our outcomes and take matters into our own hands is hard to resist. Our imperfect nature falls short every single time. If we were perfect, we would not need a savior. I am thankful that someone is above all this and is in control. He wants to rise to be the most prominent relationship in your life. His name is Jesus. God sent him to give us an eternal life. Jesus has all authority in heaven and on earth, which makes him above all things. He desires to give you and me a life complete with faith, hope, and the greatest of all, love.

Knowing this should help us lean on Jesus and trust, he has all our problems in his hands. He oversees it all and has the last word on everything. Let us resist our human nature to look around at our problems and surrender them all to the one Jesus, above all things.

Prayer: My God, help me look up and see you. You know everything I need, and you alone are above it all. You are with me. In Jesus' name, Amen.

*Date*_____

What I am thankful for

today:_____

_____

_____

_____

_____

_____

_____

My personal

prayer:_____

_____

_____

_____

_____

_____

_____

YOU WILL MAKE IT

Being confident of this, that he who began a good work in you will carry it on to completion until the day of Christ Jesus.
Philippians 1:6

Basketball is a team sport about shooting a ball into the defender's hoop. The best shots are the ones that go in smoothly without bouncing and make a swoosh sound through the net. The audience cheers extra loud. Yet, we realize there is more to the game, and only one team can win. The ball must go through a ton of passes, skips, fouls, kicked, and taken away by the other team. Eventually, it gets back in play, and upon the player's ability, it makes it into the net and scores. The team with the highest scores wins.

Our lives are comparable, even while we have a relationship with Jesus. There are days when we feel bounced around, kicked, and stolen from. It takes perseverance for us to get back on track. We all want to be winners in life. Life is tough, but you will win when you surrender everything to Him. Please do not give up, and you will make it.

Prayer: My God, help me to embrace you in every area of life fully, and I thank you for carrying me through all the twists and turns of life. I choose to trust the work you are doing in my life.
In Jesus' name, Amen.

*Date*_____

What I am thankful for

today:_____

_____

_____

_____

_____

_____

_____

_____

My personal

prayer:_____

_____

_____

_____

_____

_____

_____

_____

START WITH THE DISHES

The Lord is my strength and shield; my heart trusts in him, and he helps me. My heart leaps for joy, and with my song, I praise him.
Psalm 28:7

One morning, I felt overwhelmed with the daily tasks ahead of me. There is always so much to do and so little time. Running a business, kids, house, and family is all so consuming. I am sure you have felt the same way, but what do we do about it? Completely frozen on what to work on, I heard the Holy Spirit say quietly, "Start with the dishes." God? I questioned. Is this all I need to do? So, I did. I started cleaning my dishes and completed all my tasks the rest of the day without hindrances. My day was like a cool breeze and a drink of cold water on a sweltering day. God carried me through my day.

God is faithful to meet us right where we are and cares about our daily duties. Whatever that first step looks like for you today, take it and allow the presence of the Holy Spirit to work out the rest of your day.

> **Prayer:** My God, help me not to feel overwhelmed today, and show me my priorities. Thank you for grace in every detail of my life. Please give me the courage and strength to get through my day.
> In Jesus' name, Amen.

---

*Date*_____

What I am thankful for

today:_____

_____

_____

_____

_____

_____

_____

_____

My personal

prayer:_____

_____

_____

_____

_____

_____

_____

_____

FEAR NO EVIL

Even though I walk through the darkest valley, I will fear no evil, for you are with me; your rod and your staff, they comfort me.

Psalm 23:4

Growing up in an unstable, divorced Christian home, I did not know I was a breeding ground to be afraid of terrible things happening to me and the ones I loved. Nothing seemed to go right growing up, which led me to carry childhood fears into adulthood. Even though I am a Christian, I was living with anxiety because of my fears. Then, without realizing it, I would carry this onto my loved ones and cause them anguish. One morning, during my prayer time, I felt free from fears and finally understood what was causing them. Jesus is with me, and I should fear no evil! His rod and staff for my protection and comfort! These are word pictures of a shepherd fighting off dangers with a rod to protect his sheep and a staff to guide the sheep. Jesus is my shepherd. I am still a work in progress, and I do my best to remember that my security comes from Him. I hope you remember Jesus is with you and that there is no reason to fear.

Prayer: My God, thank you for being my protection and comforting me. I ask for your presence in my life and power over all evil. Please help me do my best to be courageous because you are with me.
In Jesus' name, Amen.

*Date*_____

What I am thankful

for:_____

My personal

prayer:_____

ROAD SIGNS AND MAP

Your word is a lamp for my feet, a light on my path.
Psalm 119:105

As you know, when traveling to unknown places, to find your way, there are road signs, maps, or, nowadays, the most used GPS will get you to your desired location. I am thankful for the use of a GPS. When you take a wrong turn or get lost, the GPS will guide you back in the right direction.

The Bible is our GPS, a living document that leads us with signs and directions and has every answer for our lives. Anytime you feel off track and not heading on the right path, this book with the holy spirit in your life has the answers. The words in the Bible are God-breathed, but we need to read them, or our lives can steer off course. God is graciously waiting for us; he will not force us to turn towards Him. Once we understand this, we can self-correct and see God turn things around for good. The Bible is our GPS to live by!

Prayer: My God, I will surrender my life to you and keep me heading in the right direction so I will stay on the path you have planned for my life. In Jesus' name, Amen.

*Date*_____

What I am thankful for

today:_____

_____

_____

_____

_____

_____

_____

My personal

prayer:_____

_____

_____

_____

_____

_____

_____

OPERATION JOY

Until now you have not asked for anything in my name. Ask and you will receive, and your joy will be complete.

John 16:24

My husband and I have been running a business together for years. We had an emergency when my husband, who is an electrician, severely injured his right shoulder and needed surgery. We had to close our electrical company for weeks. It was tough for me to be happy during this time, and I was falling into depression. I was facing tough decisions. The Bible says joy comes in the morning, and one morning, I woke up and realized this lack of joy needed to change. It was time for an emergency operation for joy.

The tools needed to be joyful again are to worship, read the Bible, pray, and seek God. The Bible says we have not because we ask not. Ask God where he would have you make changes and ask Him to give you the desired joy. He promises that if we ask, our joy will be complete. We do not always have to be happy with life's circumstances, but we can feel joyful again after the operation of Joy that only comes through knowing Jesus!

Prayer: My God, help me use the operational tools I need for Joy: prayer, reading your Bible, being grateful, and serving others to feel complete in you. In Jesus' name, Amen.

*Date*_____

What I am thankful for

today:_____

_____

_____

_____

_____

_____

My personal

prayer:_____

_____

_____

_____

_____

_____

_____

OUR WEAKNESSES HIS STRENGTH

But he said to me, "My grace is sufficient for you, for my power is made perfect in weakness." Therefore, I will boast all the more gladly about my weaknesses, so that Christ's power may rest on me.
2 Corinthians 12:9

We all have areas of our lives that we are weak in; one of mine is writing. I attended ten different schools and needed a proper education. Grammar has always been a challenge for me. About ten years ago, I felt the holy spirit nudging me to write devotionals. I was fearful and completely shocked. How is this happening to me? But the words and thoughts to write would not disappear, and new opportunities to use this new gift started presenting themselves. What do the areas of weaknesses look like in your life? Weaknesses in our personalities and capabilities are familiar to everyone.

This bible verse speaks directly to us: His grace is sufficient, and His power is perfect in our weakness. It even goes as far as telling us we boast more gladly about our weaknesses. If it were in our strength, then God would not need to be a part of our lives; it draws us closer to a relationship with him. Are you thankful that God works through your weaknesses? His ways are perfect!

Prayer: My God, help me acknowledge and surrender my weaknesses to you so that your power can rest perfectly in my life. In Jesus' name, Amen.

*Date*_____

What I am thankful

for:_____

_____

_____

_____

_____

_____

_____

My personal

prayer:_____

_____

_____

_____

_____

_____

_____

HOLDING ON TO TIGHT

Now to him who can do immeasurably more than all we ask or imagine, according to his power that is at work in us.
Psalm 28:7

Do you want to hold on to people or manipulate situations that are not in your realm of control? Are you afraid that something terrible will happen if you lose control? If you have seen the Disney movie, Finding Nemo? The father fish feared losing his son because he lost his wife, so he was overprotecting the son and did not want him going out into the vast ocean, afraid of losing him too. He was living in the pain of his past. Does this speak to you as it does to me? It indicates why we hold tight and do whatever we can to control the outcomes.

Faith is about complete trust in God, knowing his ways are higher. But letting go so God can gain control is difficult and takes practice. Even if something terrible happens, he faithfully brings you through it. So, either way, it is a win-win. The Finding Nemo movie concludes with Nemo and his father reconciling and achieving freedom. So, whatever you feel you want to control, choose to let go, trust in God, and let Him show you everything will work out for good.

Prayer: My God, please give me peace as I let go of my tight hold on something I have no control over and trust that everything will be better than ever. Help me understand everything belongs to you, anyway. Thank you for healing me from my past so I can let go of my future and place it in your hands. In Jesus' name, Amen.

*Date*_____

What I am thankful for

today:_____

_____

_____

_____

_____

_____

_____

My personal

prayer:_____

_____

_____

_____

_____

_____

_____

COACH

But the advocate, the Holy Spirit, whom the Father will send in my name, will teach you all things and will remind you of everything I have said to you.
John 14:26

Jesus was the Person who sent the followers out to spread the message of the Gospel. He gave them a position to cast out evil spirits and lay hands on the sick. Jesus told His disciples the best way to follow Him. He showed them how to lead, love their neighbor, forgive, and serve others, and what true faith is.

In the most genuine significance of the word, Jesus was their coach. He prepared them for what was to come. Jesus told his disciples I will ask the Father, and he will give you another advocate to help and be with you forever. The Holy Spirit came to teach us after Jesus sacrificed his life on the cross. The Bible explains that the Holy Spirit is God, and his coaching style is unique for each of us. The only thing needed is to open our hearts to His coaching and receive Him. Will you allow the Holy Spirit to come in and teach you today?

Prayer: My God, I thank You for sending the Holy Spirit to coach me in all areas of my life. From this moment forward, the Holy Spirit is my personal coach. I position myself as a student of the Holy Spirit, who is my divine coach. In Jesus' name, Amen.

*Date*_____

What I am thankful for

today:_____

_____

_____

_____

_____

_____

_____

My personal

prayer:_____

_____

_____

_____

_____

_____

_____

FAITH STEP

And without faith, it is impossible to please God because anyone who comes to him must believe that he exists and that he rewards those who earnestly seek him.
Hebrews 11:6

Faith is believing and trusting in God that he is our ultimate source of provision—complete dependence on his love and goodness for our lives. While we seek him first in everything we do, he promises we will find Him.

Over twenty years ago, we had a new baby boy and quit our full-time jobs. We had prayed and asked God for wisdom to start an electrical contracting business. It was a giant leap of faith. We had yet to determine if we would have a customer each day or work from one week to the next. Would customers call us back? Will we be able to pay our bills? It was the fear of the unknown.

We knew we needed God's help and could not sustain our business without Him. And honestly, it felt like a step of faith was the only option. After 20-plus years, we have seen God's favor in all aspects of our business and lives. What faith step will you take and trust that your heavenly Father is with you? He will do all that he has promised!

Prayer: My God, I believe in you. Help me have faith that you are with me every step of the way. I want to keep you first in all I put my hands to, and I will see your provisions unfold in my life. In Jesus' name, Amen.

*Date*_____

What I am thankful for

today:_____

_____

_____

_____

_____

_____

_____

My personal

prayer:_____

_____

_____

_____

_____

_____

_____

SANDWHICHED IN BETWEEN HIS LOVE

You go before me and follow me. You place your hand of blessing on my head.
Psalm 139:5

If, like me, you have made or had real messes to clean up in life. Have you always sensed God longing to have a relationship with you throughout your life? Have you felt him holding you but never ultimately acknowledging him? He has been behind you and wants to go before you. The Bible tells us that Jesus is the bread of life.

He is good news for your life and mine. If you believe in Jesus and ask Him to forgive you of your sins, Jesus will faithfully forgive you and has promised eternal life. You no longer need to labor to clean the messes of your life because he wants you to depend on Him to make your life clean. The Bible says Jesus makes us white as snow (1 Peter 1:19). Jesus loves you so much and longs to be your daily Bread by believing in Him. He is going before and after you, your source for a blessed life. While we seek him first in everything we do, he promises we will find Him. His hands of love are around you like a sandwich!

> **Prayer:** My God, thank you for loving me. Help shape me into someone who pleases you in all the areas of my life. Please be behind me and go before me each day. In Jesus' name, Amen.

*Date*_____

What I am thankful for

today:_____

_____

_____

_____

_____

_____

_____

My personal

prayer:_____

_____

_____

_____

_____

_____

_____

CAST YOUR CARE

Cast your cares on the Lord, and he will sustain you; he will never let the righteous be shaken.
*** Psalm 55:22***

If you have been a Christian for a while, depending on Jesus in every area of your life is what you desire to do. Still, it is difficult to remember when unfortunate circumstances repeatedly happen to cast our care to the Lord. Our natural tendencies are to solve problems with our strength and take matters into our own hands.

Casting our cares to Him is a choice we must make daily, week after week, and month after month. It may not be overnight, and it takes discipline, but slowly, you will see changes and your prayers answered. Then, with time, casting care back to the Lord immediately becomes easier when negative thoughts return.

Today, I encourage you to cast whatever is heavy on your heart onto Jesus by praying to Him. We have a faithful heavenly Father who loves us and has promised to work everything out for our good and his purpose. So, each time you feel tempted to take matters into your own hands, remember God cares for you and wants to sustain you in all areas of your life. Cast your care!

Prayer: My God, help me cast my cares on you, for you care for me. I trust you know everything, and you will work everything out according to your will for my life.
In Jesus' name, Amen.

*Date*_____

What I am thankful for

today:_____

_____

_____

_____

_____

_____

_____

My personal

prayer:_____

_____

_____

_____

_____

_____

_____

LIGHT OF THE WORLD

When Jesus spoke again to the people, he said, "I am the light of the world. Whoever follows me will not walk in darkness, but will have the light of life."

John 8:12

Have you heard the saying, there is a Light at the end of the Tunnel? Going through times in our lives that are consumingly dark, constant worry, fear, and uncertainty surround us. The pain feels so fresh that you wonder if you will ever see the light of day again. There is hope, and his name is Jesus; the saying that there is a light at the end of the Tunnel is full of truth. Jesus is the truth, and the bible says if we believe in him, we will know the truth, and the truth will set us free.

Jesus came into the world to cast out darkness, and whoever follows him will not walk through a season of darkness without a way to see out. Darkness cannot overcome the light. If you know Jesus as your savior, then Jesus will guide you through any darkness and light the way. Do you feel like you have lost hope? Ask Jesus to be the light of your life today. He is the light of the world!

Prayer: My God, thank you for being the light of the world. Please remove any darkness that wants to discourage me, comfort me. You are the prince of peace. Let others see your light through me. In Jesus' name, Amen.

---

*Date*_____

What I am thankful for

today:_____

_____

_____

_____

_____

_____

_____

My personal

prayer:_____

_____

_____

_____

_____

_____

_____

STAGNANT WATER

"Let anyone who is thirsty come to me and drink. Whoever believes in me, as scripture has said, rivers of living water will flow from within them."

John 7:37-38

Walking past a body of water with no freshwater flowing into it for a long time will be murky, smelly, mossy, and full of bacteria and diseases. The water has become stagnant and has no growth. Nothing about that water says life. What about walking past a flowing stream with fresh water flowing in and out? Does it look full of fresh fish? You will want to have a drink or jump in and swim. It looks so refreshing, fun, and full of life. The difference in our lives is the same way it has life or not, with Jesus or without Jesus. Even if you have everything this world offers, you can still feel empty, unsatisfied, and stagnant.

Jesus wants to give you a fresh drink of water, not physically, but spiritually. The gift of living water (Holy Spirit) can only come through knowing Jesus. If we allow him into our hearts and worship him daily, we will no longer be stagnant but will have a life that he died to give because He will always be the living water. Jesus is the living water!

Prayer: My God, forgive my sins, and refresh me with life and goodness today so that I may grow and be full of life and have it more abundantly. In Jesus' name, Amen.

*Date*_____

What I am thankful for

today:_____

_____

_____

_____

_____

_____

_____

My personal

prayer:_____

_____

_____

_____

_____

_____

_____

PRECIOUS REAL ESTATE

Finally, brothers and sisters, whatever is true, whatever is noble, whatever is right, whatever is pure, whatever is lovely, whatever is admirable-if anything is excellent or praiseworthy- think about such things.
Philippians 4:8

Any real estate investment has a portion of the risk attached to it. If we research before purchasing the property, we should understand whether we will gain or lose profit. The goal of real estate investments is to make a profit over a specified period. Why buy if we have nothing to gain long term? The Bible talks about our minds and there is tremendous value in our thoughts. Our mind is precious real estate, and God knows we can lose our lives based on how we invest in our thoughts.

The world has ways to keep our minds off holy things. Thinking unholy thoughts creates risks in our decisions and negatively affects our lives. The Bible says if anything is praiseworthy, think about these things. We need to control our thoughts with the help of the Holy Spirit, and over time, this investment to keep our thoughts on good things will have long-term positive effects and will profit our lives.

Prayer: My God, help my thoughts to invest appropriately and profit in my life. I want to discern what is correct, acceptable, and perfect and please you in all I do. In Jesus' name, Amen.

*Date*_____

What I am thankful for

today:_____

_____

_____

_____

_____

_____

_____

My personal

prayer:_____

_____

_____

_____

_____

_____

_____

WORSHIP ABOVE THE NOISE

Come, let us bow down in worship, let us kneel before the Lord, our maker.

Psalm 95:6

Our lives are full of busyness, interruptions, emotions, stress, tiredness, health, and financial problems. There is tremendous noise around us all the time. If you live in a city with traffic noise, the country with animal noises, or the suburbs with sirens. Wherever we are, there is noise. Finding that peaceful place in our lives with no noise is complex. When my babies were little, crying, I would turn up the worship music louder than their cries, and they would immediately stop crying. We have a natural enemy (Satan) out to cause anything that would keep us from worshiping God. Our thoughts can become so overloaded that they manage us instead of us managing them.

This is the point at which we want to stop and begin worshiping above all the noise. Turn on music that worships God, read the bible and pray. This will turn the focus away from the noises of this world and turn it towards the one that has overcome the world. Jesus is our peace for anything we have going on in our life. The noises become silent, and His ways for us become louder as we worship. Take time to worship today!

Prayer: My God, give me the strength to worship above the noise. I want to be closer to you through every area of my life and feel the peace that only comes from you. In Jesus' name, Amen.

*Date*_____

What I am thankful for

today:_____

_____

_____

_____

_____

_____

_____

My personal

prayer:_____

_____

_____

_____

_____

_____

_____

LOOK TOWARDS JESUS

Looking to Jesus, the founder, and perfecter of our faith, who for the joy set before he endured the cross, despising the shame, and is seated at the right hand of the throne of God.

Hebrews 12:2

Where are you looking? A criterion for being a follower of Jesus is keeping our eyes on him rather than life's storms. Recall the story of Peter and the other disciples in the boat on the Sea of Galilee; the waves and winds were perilous, and Jesus came walking on the water. Peter saw Him and said, "Lord, if it's you," Peter replied, "Tell me to come to you on the water." Jesus said, "Come." Peter climbed out of the boat and began walking. I can envision his heart being full of excitement and fear at the same time. Peter became frightened when he saw the effects of the wind. He looked around and said, "Save me, Lord." And he began to sink.

As soon as we stop looking at Jesus, our circumstances look like they will defeat us, but Jesus has his hand always held out, ready to save us. Pick us back up as soon as we cry out to him. Jesus extended his hand to Peter and caught him. Jesus said, "O you of little faith, why did you doubt? So, when you feel the temptation to doubt God in the storm, keep looking toward Jesus; he is always there to save you and keep you from sinking. Nothing is impossible for our God!

Prayer: My God, I ask that you give me the daily strength to keep looking at you and remember that you have never left or forsaken me, even during life's storms. Help me believe and not doubt the impossible. In Jesus' name, Amen.

*Date*_____

What I am thankful for

today:_____

_____

_____

_____

_____

_____

_____

My personal

prayer:_____

_____

_____

_____

_____

_____

_____

IT MATTERS

And even the very numbers of your head are all numbered.
Matthew 10:30

We often believe things we want to have, change, or achieve are less important than life's more urgent matters and significant issues. Our God loves us so much that he takes pleasure in even the smallest details of our lives. He even numbers the hairs on our heads. Is there something in your life you want God to do for you? Big or Small? Either way, it matters to God. You may have something on your mind right now that nobody knows about that is unique and specific to only you. You may feel uncomfortable sharing this with others and think it does not matter or nobody would care anyway. Feel free to talk to God about it. He cares about every detail of your life.

We are children of God, with DNA that no one else shares. Your heavenly father knows you better than anyone and is the perfect gift giver. He knows how to bless you. If it matters to you, it matters to God!

Prayer: My God, you are the God who created all things; you love me so much that you sent the best gift of all, Jesus, to die on the cross. Help me trust you with the details of my life. Everything about my life matters to you. In Jesus' name, Amen.

*Date*_____

What I am thankful for

today:_____

_____

_____

_____

_____

_____

_____

_____

My personal

prayer:_____

_____

_____

_____

_____

_____

_____

_____

SPIRITUAL MAKEOVER

Therefore, if anyone is in Christ, he is a new creation; old things have passed away. Behold, all things have become new.
2 Corinthians 5:17

We have all seen Television shows or YouTube videos where people refurbish used and worn-out homes, furniture, and cars and make them better, completely new, and more improved than before. The transformation utterly amazes us in the end. The makeover for our lives or the flip begins when we believe in Christ as our savior. All the wrong behaviors, negative friendships, and poor decisions begin to make their way out of our lives. We start to live in a completely new way than before. The Bible calls it being born again. It is the finest work of Jesus through the Holy Spirit.

This spiritual makeover has everything to do with the poor conditions of our soul, spirit, and body. The transformation of becoming a new person in Christ is restoration and healing to these areas and is a testimony of God's handy work and serves as an example for the world. All things become new in Christ, and others will stand amazed to see the makeover and want one too.

Prayer: My God, I ask today for you to be the Lord of my life, forgive me for my sins, take away all the old in my life, and make everything new. In Jesus' name, Amen.

*Date*_____

What I am thankful for

today:_____

_____

_____

_____

_____

_____

_____

My personal

prayer:_____

_____

_____

_____

_____

_____

_____

MISSING OUT

How abundant are the good things that you have stored up for those who fear you, that you bestow in the sight of all, on those who take refuge in you.

Psalm 31:19

In society today, there is a genuine fear of missing out (FOMO). FOMO is a compulsive behavior to maintain social connections and belonging. It is human nature to want to belong somewhere and desire genuine friendships. Fear is a natural emotion that various circumstances can trigger. Maintaining our connection with God is the most important. If we live for ourselves and do things that are not pleasing to God, we are not in the will of God. Life is disruptive, lonely, broken, and confusing without this connection. To connect to God is to run to Him, not away from him. The fear of God is the only fear we should have.

We should connect with Jesus daily and desire his will for our lives, making him first in all we do. He has good things stored up for each of us. He provides the perfect measure of everything we need to live a whole life with purpose and blessings. His love and grace have no limitations. You will have fullness in Jesus that supersedes anything you think you are missing out on!

Prayer: My God, I surrender my life over to you. I want to inherit all the blessings you have for me. Help me look to you and not this world. Lead me through this life so I will not miss out. In Jesus' name, Amen.

*Date*_____

What I am thankful for

today:_____

_____

_____

_____

_____

_____

_____

My personal

prayer:_____

_____

_____

_____

_____

_____

_____

INCREASE

The Lord shall increase you more and more, you and your children.
Psalm 115:14

It is in God's character to increase. He is the great multiplier; everything about God speaks of increase. The Bible tells us to plant and water, and God gives the increase. My childhood shattered, and my family comprised divorced parents, stepparents, biological, half, and stepsiblings. The traumas of my young life and believing the enemy's lies made me fearful about having a large family, thinking it would cause difficulties later. I feared increasing and keeping everything comfortable and small felt safe. In my heart, I knew this needed to change and needed to renew my mind. I began praying for an increase in my and my children's lives. I was planting and watering as much as I knew how. He told me boldly one day that I am the God of increase! I realized my fears of the future were hindering my personal growth.

What does an increase look like for you in your life? God desires to reveal Himself in whatever that is and receive glory. God has the best for my future, and yours, and an increase is one of them. He is the God of increase!

Prayer: My God, as I water and plant, you alone increase my life. Help me be open and embrace everything you want to do in and through me. All the glory belongs to you, and I give it to you. In Jesus' name, Amen.

*Date*_____

What I am thankful for

today:_____

_____

_____

_____

_____

_____

_____

My personal

prayer:_____

_____

_____

_____

_____

_____

_____

ALL GOOD THINGS

Every good and perfect gift is from above, coming down from the father of heavenly lights, who does not change like shifting shadows.
James 1:17

Have you ever doubted the goodness of God? Have you wondered if something was from God? The simple correct answer to your questions would be, is it good, and do I feel at peace? Then it came from God; of course, the opposite is true. If the answer is no, this is bad, and I do not feel peaceful. This is not from God. The enemy can also deceive us to make us think something is good, and it is not. That is why spending time in prayer and the word of God, a sound council, is so critical. When things are not going well, we quickly want to find blame in God, people, and circumstances around us; what about when things are going well? Are we quick to respond in gratitude towards God and know that every wonderful gift is from Him?

Begin looking for the surrounding good, and you will determine it is never far off. Once you find it, stay focused on it. Keep away from any distractions that steer you away from the goodness of God. God is good, and all things good come from Him!

Prayer: My God, every good thing comes from you. Please make all your goodness known to me today. Help me always be grateful for every good and perfect gift that you have provided. In Jesus' name, Amen.

*Date*_____

What I am thankful for

today:_____

_____

_____

_____

_____

_____

_____

My personal

prayer:_____

_____

_____

_____

_____

_____

_____

INTERTWINED

I am the vine; you are the branches. If you remain in me and I in you, you will bear much fruit; apart from me, you can do nothing.
John 15:5

What ties us together? It can be parents, siblings, your children, relatives, neighbors, friends, church, work, and money. So many things in our lives tie us together, we are all intertwined. This is how God created all things to work together. In science, the name is ecosystem. The definition of ecosystem is an area where one or many communities can thrive together. It is a community and life support system at its finest. We all need each other, and the major connection that brings us all together is the Holy Spirit. When we ask Jesus to be the Lord of our lives, we are now part of a bigger ecosystem of the Kingdom of God.

Everything about us comes from God's love. We cannot do anything completely by ourselves. We need God and each other to survive. We are living vessels for the Kingdom, and God chose to work through each of us. God is our principal source, and nothing is impossible for him. We are all intertwined!

Prayer: My God, thank you for all your creation. Everything has a plan and purpose. Help me remain in you all the days of my life and serve others. In Jesus' name, Amen.

*Date*_____

What I am thankful for

today:_____

_____

_____

_____

_____

_____

_____

My personal

prayer:_____

_____

_____

_____

_____

_____

_____

ABOUT THE AUTHOR

Alisha Goodman has been writing devotionals for over ten years and is thrilled to have them published as a book. Her desire to encourage others in the faith is tremendous. Alisha founded Faith Friends, a prayer group and a non-profit that helps support teen boys. She has served her community for over 30 years.

Further, Alisha has been married for 31 years; together, they have operated an electrical business in San Diego County for 23 years. She and her husband have two adult sons, a daughter-in-law, two grandsons, and two young men they mentor and are also part of the family. Alisha enjoys praying, reading the word of God, attending church, taking care of her household, being active, sewing, and spending time at the beach.

Made in the USA
Middletown, DE
28 October 2023